Finding Your *Vision* in the *D*arkness

*J*asmine D. *F*elder, MBA

FINDING YOUR VISION
IN THE DARKNESS

Copyright© 2020 Jasmine D. Felder, MBA

Motivated Minds Publishing

ISBN: 978-0-578-68519-9

All rights reserved.

In accordance with the U.S. Copyright Act of 1976, the scanning, uploading, and electronic sharing of any part of this book without permission of the publisher constitute unlawful piracy and theJt of the author's intellectual property.

IJ you would like to use material Jrom the book (other than for review purposes), prior written permission and requests for information must be obtained.
Printed in the United States of America
Motivated Minds Publishing Company

Table Of Contents

Dedication — 7

Prologue — 9

PART I
The Emotional Battle

Chapter 1 The Foundation — 13
Chapter 2 Generational Curses — 15
Chapter 3 X Marks the Spot — 17
Chapter 4 Different Paths — 21
Chapter 5 In the Storm — 23
Chapter 6 Plague vs. Promise — 27

PART II
Mirror Mirror

Chapter 7 Self-Identity — 33
Chapter 8 Forgiveness — 35
Chapter 9 Chasing After God's Heart — 37

PART 111
The Best You

Chapter 10 Worthy — 41
Chapter 11 Clear Vision — 43
Chapter 12 Brighter Day — 47

Dedication

THANK YOU GOD for this opportunity.

To my sweet A'Lani, mommy loves you! I thank God for you. I thank God that you are mine and I am yours. You motivate me to become the best version of myself. I promise to love you and work extremely hard to give you the best life!

To my wonderful mother, Glenda (Donna), thank you for raising me. Thank you for being everything I needed. You pushed me to be great and I thank God for you. So many times, I wanted to give up, but you pushed me to prevail. Everything I am is because of you and I thank God for you. Thank you for loving me and always having my back. I love you and I hope I continue to make you proud.

To my darling grandmother, Anna Mae I love you! Even though you may never know of this accomplishment I know you are proud of me. I am glad to still have you in my life and heart. Thank you for being my very heartbeat. Alzheimer's may have you mentally but, it will never take your heart from me.

Last but not least, to my darling sister Shakina, I pray as you sit in Heaven I have and I continue to make you proud. I love you.

Prologue

BEING HOMELESS, DEATH of a loved one, financial problems, divorce, failed relationships, and mental exhaustion, just to name a few, are all life-changing events. These events either make or break you. Life has a way of bringing some of its most challenging moments to you all at once. Sometimes the challenges can make it so hard for you to breathe. The tears, the aches, and the pains all seem like they will not end. I have been there, and if I am honest, I am probably still easing out of my own storm. If this is you, you feel the pressure, yet there is something in you holding on or even if you are tired and you do not know where your breakthrough will come from, this is the book for you. I am writing for YOU. I AM YOU!

Here I sit in the year 2020. I am a mother, a daughter, an educator. I sit with two degrees and now working on a third degree. I have finally gotten to a point where I can finally see my accomplishments and I am proud of the woman I have become. Work is still to be done, but life has challenged me and out of these challenges, I have come out shining. The question is, how did I get here? Was my path easy? Did I ever give up? Did I ever give in? Did I stop believing? Did I question God? Was I depressed? And did I ever say I wish the sadness would end? YES! Yes, I did! There was a time; I believed life would not get better and that I would always be unhappy. I craved for someone to say I see you, I notice you, and everything will be alright. For some reason, I was thought to be a human, everyday superwoman. People from family, friends, and even strangers would watch me and think, "oh, she can handle it," "she is fine," "no worries she has it." Meanwhile I was drowning in stress and wondering how I would get it done. Now that the sun has peaked its head out, I can see a little clearer and my journey makes more sense.

Throughout my young years of life, I can honestly say that I am blessed. I have gone through my shares of ups and downs, but I know that people go through worse. Now please do not get me wrong; my journey, tears, and disappointment are not to be taken lightly either. My focus is to get anyone and everyone reading this to see that you can make it through the darkness. We ALL can face the darkness head-on. The darkness I am referring to is events in life that try to drain you. The problems differ from person to person, but the situations all come from the same source. This darkness I am referring to tries to take away from you and it even makes you question your sole purpose. How do you find your vision when you cannot see your way? See, I am here to tell you my story and possibly, just possibly help you see that your storm, your darkness, and your problems can be conquered as well. Your purpose, the reason for your very being, may be hidden but it is not lost. We are about to embark on a journey where self-identity is key. My hope is that after this book you know exactly who you are. You will not have it all together because no one truly does. However, you will have the tools and recipes needed to get you past the place of hopelessness and confusion.

Lets find your vision and who God wants you to be!

PART I

THE EMOTIONAL BATTLE

Chapter 1

The Foundation

Before there can be anything, there has to be a foundation; whether the foundation is weak or solid, there is always a beginning. Growing up, I thought that I had life all figured out, funny, right? Here I am a little girl probably no older than 11 or 12, and I thought that I had already worked out my life up until 30 years of age. What I did not know at the time was that life would throw so many curve balls my way and that every time I thought I knew what was coming next, there would be a completely different scenario. You see, not only am I living a life completely different from what I expected at 12 years old, I am also living a life completely different from where I was years ago. I have truly grown and while I am still a work in progress, the once confused, not confident, and no purpose young girl has vanished. I have learned to set high expectations for myself, I am not afraid to be myself, and I trust the plan that God has for me.

| **Finding Your Vision in the Darkness**

When I think about who I was just a few short years ago, I cringe. I cringe because I was so lost. I was afraid to step out on faith. I wanted to make others happy and as long as they were happy, that is all that mattered. I could not find my passion because honestly, I could not tell you what I wanted as a young woman. My foundation was weak and at that point in my life, I had no one to lean on but God. I love my mother and grandmother and I thank God for them; a matter of fact, after God, they are the only two people who have been consistent in my life. However, without God, there is no them. So at that time, I felt alone because I already had a weak foundation. In addition to this, my foundation became weaker because I had given off pieces of my already weak foundation to people who did not deserve it. I was trying to give away a love that I did not have. I was giving away a love I knew nothing about. I was trying to give away a love I had not seen.

So the question is, could I give away something I did not know about? Would it bring pain? Definitely! As the cliché says, I was looking for love in all the wrong places. See if you are like me; we find pleasure in making others happy, especially the people we care about. We go above and beyond to give others peace and joy that we may not have ourselves. In doing this, we take the risk and place ourselves in jeopardy of getting hurt. No one but, God can help you build your foundation the right way. When you get to know God, you will truly find who you are. God is our foundation! He is the one who seals every crack and fills every hole. To truly know ourselves, we have to know him. Once we are aligned with God, our progress begins.

CHAPTER 2

GENERATIONAL CURSES

Now that I am a parent, I understand just how important parents are. The role we play in our children's lives lasts for an eternity. As a parent, it is our job to take care of our children, protect them from any and all hurt or danger, and guide them on the right paths. Many times our children detour a lot from what we tell them, but when you train up a child in the way they should go, the values always stay with them.

As an adult, I realize now that my childhood had many toxic factors that still affect me as an adult. My mom and dad should not ever have been together except for the moment in creating me. They were not good for each other, and the toxicity of their relationship spilled into me. I realize now as an adult my idea of relationships are falsified due to the fairytales I watched on TV and the ones I created in my head. I did not see a good example of a man loving a woman, his child, and taking care of his household. So in return, my expectations from a relationship become heightened and even maybe sometimes

Finding Your Vision in the Darkness

become unrealistic.

We do not realize how much our childhood affects us and how our parents and their actions affect us even years later. Many people become alcoholics, drug addicts, liars, criminals, teen parents, and more solely due to their upbringing. Now, this does not mean that a great parent always produces great children, and this does not mean that parents who lack good judgment produce children who are corrupt either. It does mean that parents are the first example their children see. Their learning styles, use of language, and behavior patterns are all acquired based off their environment.

We have to educate the generation we want to witness. The adults we one day want to interact with; we have to prepare them now. While my childhood caused many late issues for me, I refuse to let the cycle repeat with my daughter. As a matter of fact, I refuse to let it repeat with me! Many individuals are subject to pain and frustration due to not knowing how to break generational curses. We speak against repeated cycles in the name of Jesus right now! It happened to your mom, but it does not have to happen to you! Your dad left? You do not have to leave your child! No one in your family has graduated from college? You can be the first!

Chapter 3

X Marks the Spot

You have to be fine in the place you are currently in, in life. It is like we want to rush through the bad times but prolong the good times. We are exactly where we are supposed to be in the timing that God wants us to be there. It is understandable that no one wants to be in that place where you are lonely, questioning friendships, or not getting one call back from the jobs you are applying to. It is truly hard to be in that bad spot, especially for a long period of time. Imagine applying for jobs you know you are more than qualified for, but every email says, "thank you for applying, but we have chosen to go with another candidate." Yes, that was me. I was unfulfilled in one career but confused about where to go next. God often does one of two things. He either one, allows challenging situations to come to eventually lead us into our destiny or two, takes a step back to allow the consequences of our actions to occur and then lead us into our destiny. The dreadful times to us are not a punishment from God, but a trial and preparation period that coaches us into our next level.

Now sometimes God knows that we are not going to do right until he lets us go through a period of fault, call it tough love if you prefer. However, when we are in the tough parts of our life, we are strangely at our best. We are vulnerable, but we are in the place where God can use us the most. Doctors, lawyers, teachers, business owners, and authors have been made from going through their own storms. Hard times typically build and generate us into the best version of ourselves. Again, God knows us and unfortunately, he knows we sometimes need a push in the right direction before we can get to where he wants us. For example, God places the vision of opening up a business into you. What is the typical response? "I am not sure about that God" or "I cannot open a business." Now here come the excuses "I do not know anything about running a business" or "I do not have the money." God hears your plea but instead of removing the vision from you, he now gives you purpose. Maybe it is in you losing your job, your child needing extra funds for college, or you needing additional income. God always gets his way and fortunate for us; he knows the way. HE IS THE WAY!

Maybe you are in your hard time right now and cannot see your way. You do not know why you have been rejected time and time again. Those who you thought were for you proved to be against you. The career, relationship, and home you spent years in have been taken away from you without a second glance. X marks the spot! You are exactly where God wants you to be. He is using this hard time to make you stronger. He sees your frustration and he hears your prayers. You may think he is not working, but he is indeed working on your behalf. You have planted the seeds and now they are about to flourish.

Do not doubt the process and do not wait in terms of rushing your storm. Wait in terms of belief and anticipation because as I tell you, I tell myself, God is about to come in clutch with a blessing. We do not see it because it is not meant for us to see, and we do not understand because it is not meant for us to understand but everything happens for a reason.

Embrace this hard time because it too shall pass but if you rush it, you will only miss the purpose of what it should have taught you. I remember I was in church one day and I heard a parable about a man and his daughter. He said that while driving through a bad storm, his daughter started to get scared but her dad told her to not worry and to keep driving. She had on her windshield wipers but they did not seem to help her. She sat up straight to help her see the road better but, this too failed her. She saw other drivers pull over to the side of the road to wait until the storm passed, but her dad stopped her. He told her to not pull over to just drive slow but steady.

Eventually, through perseverance and her dad, she was able to finally make it out of the rain and see some sunshine. After making it out of the storm, her dad told her to pull over, and the daughter said, why now and the dad says I want you to see something. The daughter pulls over and gets out of the car with her dad and her dad points out how everyone who pulled over in the storm is still in the storm but everyone who kept driving is now in the sunlight. Now I am no preacher, but the point I am making is clear as day, DO NOT STOP because you will stay stagnated. The darkness we face is hard and overwhelming, but we eventually make it with God. We all can think about a situation that at one point and time bothered, scared, or hurt us, but you made it, right? If it is not your time now, trust it will be X marks the spot because you are right where you need to be.

Chapter 4

Different Paths

What happens when your path differs from all of those around you? I cherish my friendships because I do not have many and you cannot trust everyone. I have had friendships come and go, and most friendships were only meant for a season. So the friends that I have mean a lot to me. God wants us to have relationships; that is why he created us all. We are meant to laugh, feel joy, fall in love, and have fun.

    We are born into our families and we love these individuals by default. However, our friendships are the people we choose. These are the people we assume truly understand us. We share the same likes in music, shopping, and food. Our friends are who we talk to and share some of our deepest and darkest secrets with. Some days we may even choose our friends over our family. However, what happens when you start to notice you are on your own path and your friends seem so far away? What happens when the phone calls diminish, and the outings stop? The saying says, "birds of a feather flock together." What

Finding Your Vision in the Darkness

happens when your flock seems to be different and now you all are on different paths?

Our lives change. Who we were at 20 is a different person from who we are years later. Our likes change; the people we want to associate ourselves with change. As the years go on, we should be growing and there is nothing wrong with realizing you have grown, you are different, and you want more. As you grow into who you are supposed to be and align yourself with God, you will realize you are on different paths with many people. Initially, you will feel like you are betraying your family and friends if you start to separate yourself from them. In addition to this, you may even be faulted for wanting to better yourself. However, you are not to blame for someone else's shortcomings and you are also not in charge of fixing someone else's life.

Being on different paths can sometimes be lonely. You see all of the people you once associated yourself having fun and enjoying life with. You seem to be working hard and not getting anything in return for it. Take this time of loneliness, despair, and quietness and use it to rise and better yourself. I am a firm believer that when your back against the wall and when it seems like no one is around, your very best is brought to the surface. So faint not, congratulate others in their great times, pray and stay consistent. Be confident that when your path seems abandoned, God is there and you are closer to your blessing. I have learned that your vision cannot be presented until you are closed off and alone enough to listen and receive it.

Chapter 5

In the Storm

Where did I go wrong? If I could go back, I would not have made that decision. I am pretty sure we have all asked these questions in life multiple times. If you are like me, you feel like you are a pretty decent person. You pray, you go to work every day, you do right to people, and you have a sincere heart. Yet! It seems like the people who try the hardest receive the most issues. You feel unappreciated in your relationship, you question your purpose at work, and you even start to undervalue your own relationship. After many years on your job, you are passed over again and again for a position you know you are qualified for and a position you know you deserve. You have upgraded your wardrobe, lost the extra pounds you were looking to lose and changed your overall appearance but no one seems to notice the effort. Finally, you have given your relationship everything inside of you, but your significant other still seems to be on a different mindset than you. In the midst of these tribulations, we ask God, "why"? Why must I go through this? Why must my children go through this? Why have you allowed me to get sick and AGAIN at that?

The real hurt comes when we look around and it seems as if almost everyone else seems to be thriving. It appears that people are passing you by. Your friends are getting married and starting their families while you remain single or a single parent. You have family members who may be younger than you, but they are flourishing in their careers while you remain stagnant in the same position for ten years. You have not been in a relationship for years, but people who are liars and cheaters seem to get the best people while you only seem to meet people who want to misuse and abuse you. You deserve to have a family, you deserve that promotion at work, and you deserve to be loved correctly as God has designed but it has not happened.

Of course, we say we trust God, but do our actions actually show and sincerely mean that? When praying, do we at that moment give the situation to God, or are we secretly holding on to it in case he does not move in our timing or on our terms? In the storm is where we tend to feel abandoned. In the flesh, it is only so much that we can handle so, of course, when life presents hard trials and unimaginable situations we want to run, and we wish that it was anyone else but us. While we take it personal for God, it is anything but he wants us to smile and he wants us happy. However, God knows us and he knows that the process cannot be entirely easy for us or we would not appreciate the blessing as much. God has to isolate us so that we are reminded in the end where our help truly comes from. We depend too much on friends and family, which is why according to God's plan, these same people have to disappoint us. Understand that in these moments, it is not always personal.

The disappointment that is given to us is not intentional. It is more so these people are moved out of the way so that God can work on us. We cannot hear from God if we are clouded with noise. My mother is an awesome woman and I truly thank God for her. My mother has always had a passion for helping people and being their aid so to speak in a time of need. My mother had a rough childhood and upbringing. She has felt the pains of losing a parent at an early age, feeling alone, hungry, judged, and belittled. She honestly strives to help anyone in need that she comes into contact with. Going through her own issues, she would provide financial assistance, food, and more just to ease the pain of others. However, when the same people she helped got on their feet, they would either slowly stop talking to her or just disappear altogether. It was frustrating for me seeing that I am a true protector of my mom and her good heart. I remember the day exactly that she had an epiphany of why those she helped would leave. She said God told her she was being a crutch for those individuals. He did not intend for her to either help them or help for as long as she did. She became a distraction to them and they took their eyes off of God helping them and focused on her helping them. While her intentions were good, she was not a part of the plan and God had to let her feel the pain of those individuals leaving so that she would understand to only intervene when God led her.

No matter what you are going through, know that you will get through it. Your storm is hard and very personal for you. The feeling of abandonment can be torturing and scary to face alone, but you are not alone. Your storm is specifically created for you, and there are so many blessings that are created in the aftermath of those storms.

Chapter 6

Plague vs. Promise

One would think that God has forsaken us. What other reason would there be for the constant misfortune that appears to plague our lives? Over the last decade, it seems as if so many diseases, sickness, and financial droughts have plagued the world. No longer are just older people dying away. No longer are sick people dying away. We now see young people dying from sickness and people waking up one morning but not making it home. After years of tears and heartache, I have concluded that we as a people, have put our trust in the wrong people. God meant for us to have relationships, which means that we are not condemned for loving our loved ones or wanting to grow with them. However, the problem comes when we treat God as if he is an option or a backup plan instead of the one and true loving God that he is.

God is a jealous God. We are seeing now with our very own eyes how much of a jealous God that he is. For years and decades, we have placed God on the back burner. Prayer

| Finding Your Vision in the Darkness

was taken out of schools and the church seemed to brew corruption. God has been speaking to us, and of course, we all have gotten caught up in our own lives, needs, and wants that we did not hear him or listen to him. God's wrath has come upon us and he is removing all the distractions. His removal of distractions is not a punishment, although it may seem like it. God wants us as a people and his children to come back to him and surrender. The question is, will we?

God has so many great blessings in store for us. He wants to give us the desires of our hearts, but we have to put him first. Putting him first means to have the most important relationship in our lives with him. While there seem to be plagues all around in the physical sense, we all face mental and spiritual plagues daily. Our internal emotional battles prevent us from being our very best person. They stop us from truly reaching the promise that God has for us. Our emotional battles plague our minds. They make us see the situations in our lives in ways that are not true. The idle thoughts in our mind make us think lies that are not true. The only way to win this battle is to put God first and truly surrender. Pray and pray some more! Give everything to God. His ways are not our ways and his thoughts are not our thoughts. It is ok if his plan takes a different path from what we would have preferred. It is ok if his timing is reduced or exceeds what we would have planned for it to be.

The very first task in truly finding your vision in the darkest parts of life is to win the emotional battle from within.

INTERMISSION

Have you ever been to a play or concert and they tell you we will have a brief intermission and then we will shortly return for the next act? I have, and if you have not then, please go to a concert or NBA game because you need this experience. It came to a point where I had a brief intermission in my life, where I stopped performing. I was upset because here I am feeling undervalued and underappreciated. No, I am not perfect, but I pray every day and I worship God. I am a good person; I help people; I have graduated from college, and work hard. Yet! Nothing seems to be happening the way I want it too.

I was praying every day for God to bless me with the career I wanted, the man I wanted, and for me to be happy. However, in spite of all of that, all I kept getting is no. Not even a not yet, I just kept getting no Jasmine. I cannot begin to tell you the hurt and truthfully the embarrassment I felt because I just knew I deserved to be where I wanted to be. See, one thing I have yet to explain is my sensitivity. Seeing that I view myself as a good person and I give my all to those around me, I crave for the same in return. I took every loss personal. I took every defeat in shame. I took every rejection in embarrassment. The great thing about intermissions is they do not last. Eventually, the next act has to come and eventually, everyone has to come back to their seats to enjoy the rest of the show. I am so grateful that trouble does not last always and that my brief moment of giving up did not last. Who knew these same trials would come back and be the very reasons I broke through! The losses I took personal came and provided me with a platform to win. The defeat I took in shame came back and had to kneel at my feet and provide multiple wins for me. The rejection I was embarrassed about now had to come to me and ask for my permission. God is turning it around for your good! Every setback, every humiliation, every trial, every

Finding Your Vision in the Darkness

tear WAS NECESSARY!

God wants to show us that no matter what piece of paper we have, no matter how many years we have been working, and no matter who we think we are, he is the only one who can help us. So many times, we get distracted and think that as long as we do what the world sees as successful, we will be. The intermission part of our lives is a symbolic way of explaining our journey. This is the crossroads part where God has taken us through some hard journeys. He has allowed us to feel the good and bad times. He has shaken us and now he is ready to shape us into our destiny. However, this intermission is a momentary break time to ask ourselves, "are you ready?" Have you looked at your foundation, are you ready to listen to God's instructions, and have you separated yourself to embark on your destined journey?

The hardest part is letting go and sometimes anguish means you are moving in the right direction. Again, before a vision can be found, you must know yourself, you must trust yourself, and you must be accepting of God's direction.

Part 1 was meant to be an emotional battle. The truth is only revealed when you can admit your deepest feelings off the surface. As we embark on part 2 of this journey, you will begin to shed the parts of you most people wish to keep hidden. Part two is established as You vs. You. Will you do what is necessary to remove the tainted factors of your life?

MIRROR MIRROR

Chapter 7

Self-Identity

Who are you? Are most of us able to answer this question and if so, can we answer it truthfully. I do not mean in terms of what your name is, how old you are, and what is your favorite color? These are the typical on the surface questions asked and the answers we give. I want to know who are you? What are your goals? Your dreams? Your long-term plan in life? What is your life's mission statement? These questions and the answers that we provide are who we truly are.

The journeys that we take in life mold us to our very own self. Many of us face identity issues of not knowing who we are to not knowing what we should do in life solely because we are trying to mold ourselves. We want to be just like our big sister, a celebrity, or some stranger that we saw. We never understand that what works for one person may not work for the other or the simple fact that we do not know the ins and outs of everyone's life. Self-identity is taking the time to know yourself. I believe we all can agree that we have gone on journeys unnecessarily and taken the wrong routes in life simply due to not knowing ourselves. I myself have made choices seeing that at the time, maybe it seemed correct because others were making the same choice. As I look back, I can see so much of the time I spent being saved if I had consulted God before making decisions. Had I prayed about the career that was for me and had I prayed for the right people to be in my life, I would not have gone through the unnecessary pain.

Finding yourself is one of the greatest aspects of life. Knowing who you are, what you will stand for, and what you are called to do provides a peace that is not understood until you find it. The recipe to finding your true self is simple. It starts with having expectations and sticking to them! There are many people who will question you and have different beliefs from you. That is ok! The difference in opinions is ok but never let anyone make you feel bad or delusional because you have standards. After setting your expectations and sticking to them, it is imperative to remove anything and anyone who does not provide you with peace. This is a tricky one, right? Honestly no, remove all things that take away your peace in a negative way. Now I do not mean your mom made you mad, so cut her off or you and your significant other are working through growing pains. I mean that person or situation that does not grant you peace at all. While you consistently give give give, they take take take. While you are putting in the work and proactively trying, they belittle you for your attempts and tear you down. This is the negativity that must be eliminated before you can find your inner peace and true self. Self-identity is one of the most challenging phases of life because while we all think we know ourselves, but we lack the commitment to truly understand our inner self.

Chapter 8

Forgiveness

The biggest test of them all is forgiveness! This is the level that will show your growth without you ever having to say anything. There are two parts to forgiveness; there is the part of you that wants to forgive and says that you have forgiven that person or situation. The second part of forgiveness is that part of you that has forgiven or is struggling with the act of truly letting go of the hurt and pain of forgiving.

Forgiveness is such a powerful action and many of our lives are tainted because we have not forgiven someone and we are holding on to that anger, sadness, or feeling of betrayal. Forgiveness is required to elevate. You cannot move on and prosper in life while holding onto hatred because if you do not forgive those unresolved feelings turn into hatred. I am sure as we have all heard, forgiveness is not for the other person, but it is required for you to move on. Whether you are holding on to the pain publicly or in your subconscious, it still hurts you, it stagnates your growth, and it bruises you. The unforgiveness begins to turn rotten inside of you and it hinders your growth.

Some of us have unforgiveness in our hearts and we are blocking our own blessings because we cannot get over our past. Someone is missing their husband or wife because they cannot get over the hurt of a failed relationship, someone is missing the career they should have because they are angered that they did not get the job they wanted, and my favorite is a beautiful woman who cannot receive the love her man so desperately wants to give her because she cannot get over the hurt and pain that her daddy left behind years ago. I speak for you, my sister and my brother because if we continue to hold on to the past, we will remain there. There are people around the world who are still holding on to a situation that happened over 20 years ago because they have not been taught how to forgive.

Forgiveness does not mean reconnection. You can forgive yourself and move on with your life in true happiness. However, in order to truly forgive, you have to dig deep and address the issue. You must bring out every issue and uncover every hidden space. Once these issues have been addressed, you can forgive and if need be, walk away from the situation. Do not let unforgiveness rob you of the life you deserve. No one is perfect and we all make mistakes. Sometimes those mistakes can be forgiven with reconnection and sometimes they must be forgiven without reconnection. No matter what, it is important to move forward and live in love and light. Jesus came so that we can have life more abundantly. This means that we are supposed to be happy and although trials may come, we are meant to live and take all of the goodness in life that God has for us.

Chapter 9

Chasing After God's Heart

I heard a saying one time that you should want to be so embedded in God's heart that anyone who wants to be close to you has to get close to God as well just to get to you. Wow. Think about that for a moment, anyone who desires a connection with you must desire a connection with God because they can only reach you by going through God first.

Chasing after God's heart is such a beautiful thing because in him do we find ourselves. Many times we face unnecessary trials because we are not embedded in God's heart. We place so much time in chasing relationships, money, careers, acceptance on social media, and the attention of others. We have forgotten that God is where we need to be and if we do not feel his presence, we are the ones who have taken the step back not God.

Our first love is God and I think many of us have forgotten this key factor in life. We are to build on our relationship with God. Building on our relationship with God includes having

| Finding Your Vision in the Darkness

daily conversations with him and consulting him for all things. The problems we have typically start when we go out and chase our own desires and needs, then we come to God when we have messed up and need him to fix what we have created. Chasing after God's heart is a continuous action meaning you desire all that the Father has for your life. You trust his judgment overall. If he wants to give you a gift, you trust him and, if he wants to take away something you think you may like or even love, you trust him even more!

God has so much in store for us! There are so many gifts that he has created within us that he wants us to enjoy. The question that presents itself to be asked. Do you want all God has in store? Are you ready for the blessings he has for you? Are you willing to take the necessary steps to get the fulfillment of your blessings? If you say you are, then continue to chase after God's heart. Trust his timing and trust his plans. Remember, God says his thoughts are not our thoughts and his ways are not our ways. This means that he does not have to give us our blessings in the ways we think he should or how we want him to. Despite the differentiation in routes, God will get us where we need to be if we faint not. I know its hard; I have shed many tears writing this book because I understand the process is hard. However, keep pushing and know all is well.

Part two encourages you to see yourself in the mirror. Part two encourages true vulnerability. Through this segment, you should have been able to be totally honest with yourself. Before you can come through the darkness, you have to be able be honest and while the truth may hurt, it is the only way to reach your destination. Keep chasing after God's heart and trust that those who mean well for you will chase after his heart with you.

Part III

THE BEST YOU

CHAPTER 10

WORTHY

Can your worth be put in a monetary form? Should it be put in a monetary form? What do you see yourself being worth if so?

I am not sure if you know but you are worth it all! When you ask yourself, am I worth this? Or you say well because of my past; maybe I do not deserve this blessing. Remove all of those thoughts. No matter where you have been or what you have done the moment you decided to do right, God forgave you. Many of us have come from backgrounds or environments that tell us you cannot be a doctor, being a part of the judicial system makes you a snitch, playing football in the hood does not make you a star, or writing in your notebook is not equivalent to being an author. However, realize that everyone cannot see above the glass ceiling and everyone does not have a vision. You can and YOU WILL with hard work conquer your goals!

Our worth is not determinant on how much money we make, our physical characteristics, or what people think of us. Our worth is determinant on our spiritual characteristics, our

Finding Your Vision in the Darkness

right doings, our personality, and our heart. The good part of us! You may have just come out of a very toxic relationship. You had to give up the home, you do not have a car, and you received a demotion on your job. Physically and financially, it seems like all is lost and to the average person, your worth may seem less. However, with coming out of your bad situation, you found your voice, you learned how to save your money, and most importantly, you are happy. It may seem like you lost but honestly, you gained and what you gained no one can take away! Knowing your worth is so crucial as you come out of the darkness seeing that in the beginning, it may be hard to physically see the blessings but, when you tap into the spiritual mind, you will be able to see all God has given you.

You are worth the conversation; you are worth the apology, you are worth the date night, you are worth the promotion, and more! Do not take less because someone wants to give less. Their lack of commitment and understanding does not dictate your worth. Do not ever confuse unwillingness with unworthiness. You have arrived, be proud of the person you are now. No, you may not be where you want to be but the mere fact that your mental state has began to change is enough reason to praise God. Every time someone makes you question your worth or makes you feel as if you are asking for too much follow this acronym.

W- are they **W**illing to try?

O- have they **O**ffered to try?

R- is this **R**eally what I want?

T- am I being **T**rue to myself?

H- am I truly **H**appy?

Y- do they make me **Y**ield to my desires?

Chapter 11

Clear Vision

*F*inding your Vision in the Darkness is catered to helping you have a clear vision. We often do not have a clear vision because we cannot hear from God. We know what time Love and Hip Hop come on; we do not miss a segment of the Rickey Smiley Morning Show, and we attend every Friday night football game, but we say we cannot hear from God. So many distractions in our lives prevent us from truly hearing what God tells us to do. God's voice does not have to be an audible sound. It could be the discernment we feel in our spirit on whether or not to make a decision.

What is your vision? What has God laid on your heart to do? What mission has he challenged you to take? Sometimes it will not feel good and often, our visions seem unrealistic to others. When I wrote my first chapter of this book over four years ago, I told people that I was writing a book and the responses I received made me doubtful. However, now through much trial and tribulation here, I am completing the vision God has set forth for me. It will not always be easy, and

| Finding Your Vision in the Darkness

everyone will not always believe in you. Also, every vision is not a task that is set to be completed quickly. Slow and steady wins the race, trust your vision, listen to God's voice. What is yours is meant to be yours and delayed does not mean denied.

I know at times when God gives us a vision, we want to tell the world. We want to share with our family and friends. We want people to believe in us just like God does. The problem with that is no one knows us like God, which means they do not know our potential like him. When starting your business, writing your book, or building your brand, it is ok to not tell anyone! It does not mean you do not believe in your vision; it just means you understand everyone does not need to be apart of every step of your journey. I have learned that not all people have tunnel vision and that is ok. What may seem too much or too hard for others does not mean it will be too much or too hard for you.

Believing in yourself is so important to the vision process. There were so many times that I wanted to give up. It seemed like the goal of writing this book was too much to accomplish. Did I really have something worth talking about? Could I inspire others? I am still a work in progress myself, so would people listen? All of these questions and more went through my head. However, I have learned who said that you have to be perfect to accomplish your goals? People need role models who are a work in progress. We are the model to show that you can be successful and great and still not have everything together. I am proof that God can take the crybabies, the illegitimate, the unpopular, the non-speakers, and compose strong warriors, legitimate owners, admired leaders, and courageous authors.

It has never been about your beginning but, more so about what you do with the pieces of life God has given you. Ok, your parents did not raise you; what can you do with that pain? No one ever believed in you, understandable but, will you use that unbelief as motivation to prosper? You were picked on in school, take those insults as compliments to push you forward. All great people have been bruised and felt pain. Instead of letting the insults and the pain keep them in bondage, they found a way to use all of the ridicule and form a better part of themselves. Never let your beginning be your ending. It is ok to cry, be nervous, be scared, and hurt for a little while. After the rain has come, USE ALL OF IT! Do not let your naysayers be your motivation because then your motives will be for the wrong reason. BUT! Promise yourself that you will not be the negative things they have called you.

Your vision will become clear when your motives are in the right place. Ask God to order your steps and let everything you do be for the Master and you will never go wrong!

Chapter 12

Brighter Day

What do you do when the darkness has subsided? Encourage your vision! Now that you have faced the past and laid it to rest, you have identified within yourself who you are and what you want out of life, and finally, you have a clear vision. As exciting as this is, the work is not quite yet done. You must encourage yourself to keep motivating yourself and speak great manifestation over your life.

Listen to me; there will be people who question you, still make a mockery of your dream, and try to make you feel bad for wanting better. DO NOT! We all are given the same amount of hours in a day, days in a week, weeks in a month, and months in a year. Despite the difference in resources, we all get the chance to be equally motivated. We choose how hard we work. So when the moment comes when someone says you are doing too much, simply say thank you. Take it as a compliment but, do not ever give up. Encourage your vision and tell yourself you can do it. When the frustrating moments come, when it seems like everything is working against you, pray. Know that

Finding Your Vision in the Darkness

God is on your side and he truly has your back.

You can smile now because you have insight. You have the dream but what are you going to do with it? Take your time and surround yourself with the correct people. Never want to be the smartest person at the table, seeing that you want to be able to give and receive. Encouraging your vision means to research and network. Step outside of your comfort and talk with people and ask questions. I would have missed my blessing of becoming an author had I not allowed God to work in my life. On what I thought was a bad day, God used it as a day to positively change my life.

Never rush or regret your storm, seeing that it builds your character. Trust in yourself and your abilities and know that all things work together for the good of them who love the Lord and are called according to his purpose. The darkest part of our lives does not feel good, but God often decides to use us in our mess. He knows that in our purest form of vulnerability, he can use us. Diamonds in a rough form is a perfect example of an excruciating situation in making a beautiful thing. I am proud of you; I am proud of us! We have already conquered the storm.

Your brighter day is here! Continue to encourage yourself. Do that very thing that scares you. Travel more, say yes to that job, do not be scared to apply to that higher position, believe in love again. Do not be afraid to let toxic relationships go no matter how long they have been a part of you. Trust God. If your relationship has wavered with him, he is waiting on you. It is not too late, come while the blood is still running warm.

I encourage you to believe beyond your wildest dreams. Yes, storms will still come, but the good part about it all is you now have the recipe for Finding Your Vision in the Darkness!

Letter to

My Readers

Wow!!! My first book! I am so happy and proud to have gone on this journey with you. About five years ago after losing my sister, God gave me this vision of writing my own book. At the time, I just shrugged my shoulders and did not think more about it. A year after that, I wrote my first chapter. Throughout the years, I would write but I still did not take it seriously. In January 2020, I felt tested in ways that made me question where my life was going. I am thankful God placed the right people and situations in my life to help me realize I had a greater purpose to serve.

This book means a lot to me because while helping you, I am taking you on a journey with me. The vulnerability that I am showing in this book is the most vulnerable I have ever been with anyone. I want you to realize that I love God with all of my heart. I strive daily to be a better person. Please understand with that being said that I am not perfect, and I am still a work in progress. I believe that is what makes me so relatable!

At the beginning of this book, we talked about what darkness is and what it means specifically for your life. We discussed the emotional battles we all face in one way or another. Each chapter includes various trials that I have faced, but in that, many of you will see yourselves. Throughout this book, you should have seen yourself in some capacity.

Finding Your Vision in the Darkness

It is my hope that through my journey, you can picture yourself and become a better person. I pray God's anointing on every word, chapter, and page of this book. I pray great manifestation among my family and your family. I pray you become the best version of yourself and you let no one steal your joy or your purpose! Greatness is on its way for you!

See you soon!

Sincerely,
JASMINE D. FELDER